Gateway to Serenity:
The Karakoram Highway

A Travel Journal

Naba Basar

Gufhtugu Publications

Reach the Author: nababasar@hotmail.com

Printed in the Islamic Republic of Pakistan.
First Printed: 2018
ISBN: 978-969-7758-14-2
Price: Rs 500 PKR, 5$ USD

Published By:
Gufhtugu Publications
Islamabad, Pakistan
info@gufhtugu.com | +92-340-4455990
Join us on Social Media @GUFHTUGU
Visit our Website WWW.GUFHTUGU.COM

Pakistan – home to breathtaking geological beauty and scintillating culture. A country with towering peaks - spectacular mountain ranges a dynamic landscape; stunning rivers, deserts, lakes, waterfalls, springs, and glaciers and impenetrable fortresses – we seem to have it all in great abundance.

Contents

Foreword

"Travel isn't always pretty. It isn't always comfortable. Sometimes it hurts; it even breaks your heart. But that's okay. The journey changes you; it should change you. It leaves marks on your memory, on your consciousness, on your heart, and on your body. You take something with you. Hopefully, you leave something good behind." - **Anthony Bourdain**

I enjoy visiting new places, meeting new people, experiencing traditional delicacies, collecting souvenirs, learning how to accommodate myself in different situations. This quote mentioned above could have easily been written by me had I traveled enough. With each trip I have taken across Pakistan I begin with a fear, an uncertainty in my heart. And I love every bit of it. Travel helps us press the edges of our perceived limitations, so that we may re-imagine them and continue to reach beyond.

I have tried to recreate events, locales, places and conversations from my memories of them. In order to maintain their anonymity in some instances I have changed the names of individuals. I may have changed some identifying characteristics and details such as physical properties, occupations and places of residence. I would also take this opportunity to thank the real-life members of the families portrayed in this book for taking me into their home and accepting me as one of their own. I recognize that their memories of the events described in this book are different than my own. They are each fine, decent, and hard-working people. The book was not intended to hurt any individual or family. Both my publisher and I regret any unintentional harm resulting from the publishing and marketing of my travel journal.

Note of Thanks: I would like to thank my broken foot to make it possible for me to write my own travelogue after 3 months of endless failed attempts.

Handy Tips
Especially if you are travelling to Northern Areas of Pakistan

- Always carry tissues / wipes / sanitizer (all 3 make a perfect combo up in the mountains!)
- Zip lock bags (small & big) / plastic bags
- Medicines especially fever / tummy ache / anti-allergy / headache / nausea for travel sickness etc.
- Bandages (for cuts) and crepe bandages (for strains & sprains) / repellent / Polyfax (a skin ointment used to treat infected wounds, burns, skin grafts, skin ulcers, itching and rashes. It may also be used to treat multiple types of skin infections)
- Olive oil / honey comes in handy for multiple purposes (to heal wounds, for stomach and throat problems)
- Biscuits or cookies which won't easily crumble / dry fruits / nuts / trail mix / mouth fresheners / sugar free gums
- Milk / cereal sachets if you are travelling with toddlers
- Cash – ATM's are not easily available and even if they are, there may be major electricity issues or non-availability of cash in certain areas
- A sturdy water bottle – nothing like enjoying fresh spring / glacier / waterfall water (no matter what people say!)
- Headlamp / Torch for emergency situations after sun sets
- Warm piece of clothing even during summers for it may get chilly after hours
- Hat / Cap and sunglasses / sunscreen – the weather conditions may intensify

- Power bank / extra phone battery (if you love taking pictures via phone) / additional camera battery
- If you happen to be around a market place when on a vacation (especially during summers), buy half kg rice! Yes, you read that right. You will soon find out why!

The Departure

The day of my departure from Karachi, weather had taken a twist and turned surprisingly cloudy and slightly windy. When it started drizzling I nervously turned to my friend, whispering prayers that the predicted downpour does not hinder our expedition before it begins.

It began with a desire: a passion to get out of the city life madness. I needed to get away from all the hustle and bustle, the crowds, the agonizing traffic, the apathy that descends upon the streets like rain, and break free from my day to day routines. I needed to flee from this commercialism that blinds people with material objects which we absently spend for in an effort to give our existence some sort of value and worth. I have always fantasized about growing up in the countryside surrounded by mountains, in a wooden cottage framed by enormous pine trees that reach for the sky. How these bitter-sweet smelling marvels stand tall.

As luck would have it the weather was great on both ends and we had a seamless flight which was an experience in itself. The monsoons had broken out a few days ago, in the twin cities Rawalpindi and Islamabad – our first destination. The blustery weather and rain were announcing their presence to the traffic as we stepped out of the deserted airport. Booking a local car service was a sensible secure selection on the 3rd day of Eid!

Though the sun had set, the market lights were hanging along the streets. Crowds of people sluggishly carried their conversations under their dark umbrellas, unlike us Karachittes enjoying the rainwater and the pleasant air.

How different the streets of Islamabad Expressway look at night, I thought as I gazed at the wide roads, and the dusky "Quaid Hill". It's a small hill that can be spotted here and bears the quote of Quaid e Azam, "Unity, Faith, Discipline", written in metallic letters in English on one side. On the other side of the hill, these three words in Urdu are "Ittehad, Eman, Nazam".

As the enchanting silhouette of Margalla hills came into view, I felt tiny butterflies in my stomach at the thought that I am finally here! I whispered to myself, Once again I am here! First stop - The Faisal Masjid!

The mosque is positioned at the northern-most tip of Islamabad on an elevated area near the scenic backdrop of the Margalla Hills. Margalla Hills is the westernmost foothills of the Himalayas.

Heading towards Pakistan's national mosque, dodging the large muddy, puddles which noticeably reflected the roadside market decorations, minus the street lights. Observing families and friends strolling in casual clothing, back and forth out of the still busy masjid pavement, it just did not seem right. Here we are standing before the iconic symbol of Islamabad world-over, which now looks like a famous picnic spot; Wrappers, empty bottles and cartons strewn all over, amidst the growing trend of 'selfies'.

Background of the grand masjid:

Completed in 1986, the Faisal Mosque (also known as Shah Faisal Masjid) is an exceptionally large and unique mosque in Islamabad. Designed by a Turkish architect who won an international competition for the honor, Faisal Mosque is shaped like a desert Bedouin's tent and functions as the national mosque of Pakistan.

The architect was Vedat Dalokay of Turkey, whose design was chosen in 1969 after an international competition. The construction was completed in 1986. The architecture is strikingly contemporary and unique, lacking both the traditional domes and arches of most other mosques around the world. The shape of the Faisal Mosque is an eight-sided concrete shell inspired by a desert Beduoin's tent and the cubic <u>Ka'ba</u> in Mecca, flanked by four unusual minarets inspired by Turkish architecture. Entrance is from the East, where the prayer hall is faced by a courtyard with porticoes. The International Islamic University was housed under the main courtyard, but recently relocated to a new campus. The mosque still houses a library, lecture hall, museum and cafe. The interior of the main tent-shaped hall is covered in white marble and decorated with mosaics, calligraphy by the Pakistani artist Sadeqain, and a spectacular Turkish-style chandelier. The prayer hall can accommodate 10,000 worshippers. (There is room for an additional 24,000 in the porticoes and 40,000 in the courtyard.)

The mausoleum of General Muhammad Zia-ul-Haq, whose 1988 funeral at the site was the largest in the history of Pakistan, is located adjacent to the mosque. *(Taken from various descriptions over the Internet)*

Finding a local taxi on a rainy night is quite a task. Especially if you are by yourself with a 5-year old, past 8pm on the road is beyond belief in Karachi. The capital city is fairly safe when it comes to being unaccompanied by a man (as I reckon). Smart thing my friend Taiba did was have our table reserved at **Monal Restaurant**. July 8th 2016 being the 3rd day of *Eid* the road to Monal was clogged. We tried our best to tell the driver *bhai* to inch a little forward, with the hope to have yummy Italian platter at my favourite restaurant. Unfortunately we did not even reach half way up the mighty hills and had to turn back before getting caught up in the traffic jam. Thanks to internet and my love for Islamabad I knew a couple of decent places to eat. ***Tuscany Courtyard*** was our savior that night. We reached the place by 10:00 pm; hungry and exhausted. The management was amazing, although the place was packed, the guy still managed to wedge us in 15 minutes later. The place smelled awesome and I secretly prayed the food would make up for our wrecked Monal trip. Personally I would give Tuscany Courtyard a 10/10 for the fantastic service, hospitality, ambience and steaming delicious food. Their desserts are a must try.

After about an hour we were headed to our tour guide's specified place. Upon reaching a quiet street with a dimly lit house, we were greeted with the most humble, courteous group of people who introduced us to Climax Adventure Pakistan's CEO & Founder Muqeem Baig's sister. Muqeem is a professional Mountain Guide, Climber & an Adventure Sports Trainer.

We freshened up...way past the midnight! We were supposed to leave the place max by 2 a.m. We signed up for the trip with these exceptionally fantastic Shimshali people. We left Islamabad as per the schedule. This being my first ever trip with a group, it was all so new, things I had imagined in my head, things I was hoping for. One of them was: Northern areas – 4x4 jeep safari for the rough mountain ride. But there was a coaster awaiting us! Never in my life I have or I could ever fancy the idea of travelling at 2 a.m. alone with my 5-year old. Islamabad somehow gives you this silent assurance that you are out of harm's way.

Story behind Climax Adventures Pakistan (CAP)

It is a Hunza-based company that operates tours throughout the many scenic regions of Pakistan, with a focus on mountaineering, trekking, camping, safaris, boating, water sports and other nature-based expeditions. Among CAP's team of exclusively skilled and experienced mountaineers are high-altitude porters who have climbed Pakistan's 8000m peaks. CAP stresses safety and has a record of no injuries.

Muqeem Baig (CEO – CAP) belongs from Shimshal valley in the province of Gilgit-Baltistan in northern area of Pakistan, "The Valley of Mountaineers".

His father Qurban Muhammad sahib worked as a mountaineer and mountain guide, who scaled many Mountain peaks in Pakistan and the first Pakistani rescue specialist. Rescued from 8000m peaks like K2, Nanga Parbat, Broad peak, Gasherbrum-I and Gasherbrum-II and saved many lives! He brought many victories for the country by flying Pakistani Flag on the summit of the world's highest Mountain Peaks. He also worked for a Hollywood film project called "The Vertical Limit" (Based on a fictitious story about climbing K2 - 1st July – 7th August 1999).

Muqeem's father's story narrated by Muqeem:

My inspiration (my father) Qurban Muhammad hailing from Shimshal valley is a mountaineer who attempted all five 8000m peaks in Pakistan and he is the rescue specialist in Pakistan. He has few records in the field of Mountaineering but here I am sharing one story.

It was July 2006 when Venezuelan climber Jose Antonio Delgado was climbing the killer mountain Nanga Parbat-8126m. Jose was stranded on C4 for an entire week after reaching the summit. Out of food, gas and with the tent destroyed by a jet storm.

Eventually Jose left his shelter and tried to descend to C3 on his own but died before reaching the camp. Rescue team members were high altitude porters, all highly experienced in 8000+ meter climbing. One of them was my father - Qurban Muhammad. Out of six rescue team members finally my father reached to the point (7400 meters) and found Jose had passed away. He passed the message to the base camp where his wife was. Frida Ayala, wife of Jose arrived in a helicopter where his body lay. She asked them to leave him there & bring his belongings back because he was for the Mountains.

Frida later held a press conference at the Ministry of Tourisms HQ in Islamabad this year and thanked the Pakistan Government, the rescue team, the expedition guides for their co-operation in the rescue attempt of her husband, and their support after the sad outcome. She added, *'If my son decides to be a mountain climber like his father, I will let him.'*

Day 01 – Journey Begins 9ᵗʰ July 2016

Plan: Departure from Lahore Friday (9:00 pm), arrival in Islamabad & join members. Continue drive from Islamabad (4:00 am) for Gilgit (14 hours), Dinner & overnight stay.

A little before 3 a.m. we reached Daewoo Express Rawalpindi – meeting point to join the other members. You will most likely start your journey from Rawalpindi. Rawalpindi is located 14km south of the capital of Islamabad, the capital of Pakistan.

My eyes were wide awake with anticipation, at this point no clue how long before we hit the road again. We waited for almost an hour for the other members to join in. Meanwhile my friend and I decided to pray Fajr before we leave. Praying in a faintly lit, mysterious corner on a damp rug was an indication that more surprises are yet to unveil.

We set out somewhere around 4 a.m. but witnessed no sunrise yet. Struggling to sleep our coaster drove in the dark not knowing exactly where we were headed. Dawn broke. The light filtered in through the curtain drawn window. As I peered out the window, witnessed magnificent hazy mountains, gushing river and the morning sunlight.

Around 9 am we reached Kiwai, just in time for breakfast. The stretch from a long night journey felt nice. The stone steps took us to the *Abshar* Café Kiwai. Refreshing as it was to experience the lavish waterfalls after a long drive up the mountains. The *Abshar* (waterfall) restaurants are a must visit. We ordered breakfast; parathas, poached eggs the *desi* way and doodhpatti, with the freezing water passing in between the toes – a delightful experience.

The last time I enjoyed this was years ago in Nathiagali, a hill station cum mountain resort town in Abbottabad District of Khyber Pakhtunkhwa, Pakistan. It is known for its scenic beauty, hiking treks and pleasant weather.

Much to our amusement was the idea of paying money for using the washrooms. Bizarre as it sounded...it was according to the time we spent in the loo! A concept I was unaware of all these years! Sadly, everything came to a halt when I accidentally dropped my dear, almost brand new cell phone in the flowing water. A loud scream and multiple instructions followed the tragic incident.

* **Tip:** If your phone / camera / sensitive equipment is not waterproof handle it with care. If you do what I did then instantly buy some rice (good thing we were close to the market place)! Bury your phone in uncooked rice and keep it in a sunny place. Leave it and it'll come back to life after 24 hours! Trust me!

Back on the road, towards Naraan – not having my phone brought my photography to an end but gave me the chance to relish the endless bounties of Allah (s.w.t.). The road to Naraan was jammed but gave us all a chance to get off and enjoy the lush green landscape, the countless beehives in boxes on the edge of the trail leading towards the mountains. And Pakistani people never miss a chance to entertain, they just need an audience. Dancing men, live performances with the local instruments, blaring music, flamboyant attire...it all jelled in well with the panorama that surround us and the moods we were in. The frequent breaks in the journey gave a chance to fill the water bottles with fresh fall water, purchase fruits, which is a healthy convenient snack.

The Kunhar River (also known as Nain-Sukh "eye's repose")

It is a 166 kilometres long river, located primarily in the Khyber Pakhtunkhwa province, northern Pakistan. It is in the Indus River watershed basin. The river originates from Lulusar Lake, nearly 48 kilometres, upstream from Naraan Valley. Waters of Dudipat and Saiful Muluk Lakes feed the river besides glacial waters from Malka Parbat and other high peaks in the valley. The Kunhar River flows through the entire Kaghan valley, Jalkhad, the Naraan valley. The River joins with Jhelum River at confluence just outside Muzaffarabad, in the Azad Jammu and Kashmir province, Pakistan. The Kunhar River is considered to have good quality trout. Trout is also produced in farms that have been developed along the river. And that's what Naraan is famous for.

*** Tip:** My advice, do not travel to Naraan during Eid holidays or be prepared to be wedged in between cars.

Our 14 hour trip turned into 24 hours. Exhausted and in a haze somewhere in the middle of the night I vaguely remember someone saying, if you want to see the stars like you have never seen before, now is your chance! We were advised to cover up as it must be -1 degrees. Dazzled by a freezing starry night sky, a view I will never forget, a feeling still electrifying!

Our journey towards Gilgit stretched to almost 24 hours from Islamabad. Jolted by emergency brakes the engine ceased. Our driver dozed off in the heart of the mountains. Between the rolling river and the shadows of the mountains someone jerked the driver up. Out of 15 of us no one realized the agony of the sleep-deprived driver. While the driver napped we got in line to use the washroom in a creepy isolated place and you end up making peace with it. Face it you do not have much choice. Incidentally Pakistanis are familiar with the concept of using all sorts of emergency lights.

We made it to Gilgit, way into the night before stopping in a deserted place for dinner. As part of our package - Accommodations: Six (06) nights Hotel on 3-4 persons sharing bases was perfect. One thing that I genuinely loved about this trip was the accommodations they provided us with all along, which were quite comfortable, secure with breathtaking morning views.

You will most likely arrive in Gilgit just after dark. Gilgit is by far the biggest town in Northern Pakistan, and you are guaranteed to stop here for at least one night. It was a very comfortable stay at ***Capital Lodge Gilgit***, with a clean decent bathroom, considered a luxury up north! Bed, clean washroom with running water is all you need after a 24 hour journey up the mountains, especially if it has both warm and cold water running! More often than not there are set timings for warm water. Here in Gilgit we stayed at another lodge – ***Heaven Lodge Gilgit*** which was beautifully structured with apple and walnut trees, blooming flowers everywhere with gushing Kunhar River flowing on one side. Accommodations in lodges, hotels, camps had been perfect throughout.

Gilgit is the transportation hub on the Karakoram Highway. It is also the only place in Northern Pakistan with ATMS that work with western bankcards too, but may sometimes be out of money. Gilgit Town itself is not much to brag about but the region is surrounded by some of the highest mountain peaks in the world. Home to Himalayas, Karakoram and the Hindu-Kush mountain ranges, Gilgit is known for its rare flora and fauna, spectacular valleys and sparkling lakes.

As we strolled looking for a place to purchase water from, I spotted The Gilgit College of Commerce and Economics Main Campus (since 2004). The tagline certainly sounded attractive:

"Preparing Mountain Business Leaders"

Day 02 – Journey Actually Begins 10th July 2016

Plan: Breakfast and continue drive to Hunza (2hrs), check in and free time.
Stopover at Silk route & Rakaposhi view point Hike up to Baltit Fort, Explore Baltit Fort & Karimabad Bazar. Back to hotel for dinner & an overnight stay.

Gilgit and Beyond

A lazy morning, a quick warm shower, and to my disbelief my phone rang amid the uncooked rice! A day without my phone ringing or buzzing was a sheer bliss in disguise. Mobile reception was better here. Northern areas are a great place to unplug partly because there are fewer places with smooth phone reception and Internet connection and frequent power cuts in many of the mountain towns. There was very little time to pack up before proceeding downstairs for breakfast.

*** Tip:** Travel light. Since you are always on the go, backpacks/ knapsacks are practical, given that they are easy to pack, easy to carry, easy to load.

It was quite a sunny day as we stepped out after our standard omelette, paratha and tea breakfast. While trying to recharge my phone in the dining hall of the lodge, I came across the tragic news of Edhi sahab's demise. He passed away 2 days back – July 8th 2016. It was definitely heartbreaking news for people around the globe. Although he was unwell for such a long time but the man had the utmost faith and courage. He lived a dignified life and died a dignified death.

As we stepped out the dry enormous mountains were clearly visible under the intense rays, bright blue sky with thick fluffy clouds hovering over the city. We never missed a chance to click pictures! By midday we left, back on a rocky road. Little did we expect to get stuck in traffic yet again!

You will observe in many places that the glacier water conveniently flows through a channel alongside the roads; the shopkeepers take the opportunity to wash and keep beverages and fruits icy cold. Fresh plump cherries and freshly cut watermelon. On a warm bright day the juicy treats were the right wholesome pick. Fruits turned out to be a perfect icebreaker between the other 10 group members' we were to travel with for another 6 days. However, at this point my fantasy remains to pick and eat fruits fresh from the orchard.

The road from Gilgit to Hunza Valley is nice and smooth with great Mountain View during the course of your journey. Gilgit-Baltistan is administratively divided into two divisions which, in turn, are divided into seven districts, including the two Baltistan districts of Skardu and Ghanche, and the five Gilgit districts of Gilgit, Ghizer, Diamer, Astore, and Hunza-Nagar. The Hunza–Nagar District was the seventh district of Gilgit–Baltistan of Pakistan. In July 2015, the district was divided into two districts Hunza District and Nagar District.

According to the Alif Ailaan Pakistan District Education Rankings 2015, Hunza-Nagar is ranked 21 out of 148 districts in terms of education. For facilities and infrastructure, the district is ranked 58 out of 148 (these statistics may vary). The main political centers are the towns of Gilgit and Skardu. These are basically famous tourist spots. Tourism is mostly in trekking and mountaineering and this industry is growing in importance.

The ride down the Karakoram towards Rakaposhi was a memorable one. A roadside signboard in Nagar

Valley identifies the spot where the Indian and Eurasian continental plates collided creating the towering mountains. **Collision Point of Continental Plates**, reads the signpost, apart from offering information about the place where the Indian and Eurasian continental plates are said to have collided almost 55 million years ago. Amazingly the Indian plate is still pushing north into the Eurasian land mass, at about 5 centimeters per year, causing the mountains to escalate about 7 millimeters annually.

In about an hour we reached Rakaposhi view point Nagar Valley, a sight I have never seen before. Under the intense gleaming sun, stood this gorgeous snow-covered peak with the most phenomenal waterfall. The long exposure of water flow from melting glacier of Rakaposhi at base camp refreshes you up on a warm day. The snow of Rakaposhi glittering in the sunlight is awe-inspiring - the water icy cold. We hiked a little, dipped our feet, clicked pictures, drank the glacial water and saved some for later.

* **Tip:** Make videos of the waterfalls and rivers you have visited. They keep the memory of certain places, moments alive. Besides very soothing to listen to especially if it's shot by you.

Rakaposhi Peak (the 27th highest peak in the world & 12th highest in Pakistan) A place I would visit again and again and again!

This mountain is in the Karakoram mountain range in Pakistan. It is situated in the Nagar Valley approximately 100 km north of the city of Gilgit. Rakaposhi means "snow covered" and Dumani ("Mother of Mist") in the local language. Rakaposhi was first climbed in 1958 by Mike Banks and Tom Patey (British Royal Navy). The best-known attraction for the Mountaineers is the North of

Pakistan. Northern part is in knot of four great mountain ranges, Himalayas, Karakorum, Hindu-kush and Pamir with densest concentration of high peaks on earth, including the second highest peak, K-2 (8611m).

Sadly with the passage of time the natural diversity of this area is threatened by anthropogenic activities. The first major glimpse that you can enjoy is from an area called Zero point (right on KKH) where you get a magnificent view of the peak, with glacier fed streams running down. Due to the mountain's distinguished position (center of the Hunza valley) many have considered climbing the peak but relatively few have attempted the summit.

If you have the time, you could also trek up to the glacier visible from the road side. Locals suggest it will take approximately 2 hours to go up there (a further 3000 - 4000 feet up). Technically it is difficult and dangerous due to extreme avalanche risk.

The place has a few very expensive shops. I am glad we waited until we reached Karimabad (Hunza) to get some fair deals. The food served was tasteful. You get an absolutely fabulous view of the snow-covered slopes of Rakaposhi, while enjoying the yummiest mountain *daal*.

* **Tip:** Savour the local cuisines. They taste and smell differently, given the diversity of the people of Pakistan; cuisines generally differ from mountain to mountain and may be different from the mainstream Pakistani cuisine you are accustomed to.

We spent a good 2 hours there before we hit the road again. Right about 20 minutes later once more we got stuck. This time the cause was an earlier landslide. With luck, the bulldozer was already pushing the boulders off the road, which gave us time to stretch, explore and take photos. Landslides are a common sight up north. The last time I experienced a mudslide in real was many years ago at Neelum River, Muzaffarabad.

Karakoram Highway (KKH) is an engineering feat where a substantial number of people lost their lives. An average of one worker died for every kilometer of road, due to landslides, heat, winter, accidents, and working in an inhospitable terrain. The road is carved through various mountains passes and is subject to landslides, especially during rainy season. Linking Islamabad (Pakistan) with Kashgar (China), the Karakoram Highway – often referred to as the 8th wonder, is one of the most epic building projects, snaking 1,200km through the Karakoram and Pamir Mountains, and demonstrating the grand vision and disregard for life that exemplifies Chinese engineering.

By evening we reached Aliabad, which is the administrative and commercial center of the Hunza–Nagar District of Gilgit–Baltistan. Aliabad lies along the Karakoram Highway, which crosses this mountainous district, like most localities in Hunza–Nagar.

Hunza – home away from home

Hunza enchanted me so much that the moment I set foot out of the coaster, I made up my mind; I could easily retire and live here. The tall slender poplar trees sway gracefully in the wind, highlighted against the snow-capped mountain in the distance, the air so pure. The apricot, cherry trees and the stone walls welcomed us and led us to our trip's finest, homelike stay ***Café de Pamir***. With a warm welcome we were lead to where we were to stay overnight, right in front of a huge apricot tree and Rakaposhi in view. We spent 2 days and 3 nights in Hunza.

Apricots - the gold of Hunza Valley

Apricot orchards are more common in Hunza and Nagar valleys, the legendary fruit of the valley. A family's economic stability is measured by the number of trees they have under cultivation. The juicy yellow fruit is the major diet in summers and dried and stored throughout the winters. The pits are cracked to obtain the kernel that is crushed to obtain the oil for cooking and for lamps. The hard shell is kept for fire fuel. The kernel and oil could be eaten from the variety of apricots with a sweet kernel, but the bitter kernel variety has oil containing poisonous prussic acid. Besides apricots, the Hunzakuts also grow apples, pears, peaches, mulberries, black and red cherries, and grapes. Mulberries, which resemble blackberries in size and shape, are a favorite fruit. When fully ripe, their flavor is sweet-sour but somewhat bland. The variety grown in Hunza is most likely a golden color - Witnessed this as we drove past the apricot laden roads, streets, hotels from Hussainabad to Aliabad to Karimabad and also caught sight of apple and cherry trees.

The warm welcome at ***Café de Pamir*** cannot be forgotten or overlooked. Freshened up as the evening clouds cleared. Taking in the view; the magical display of the ethereal mist as it appears to rise from out of the mountains.

*** Tip:** Hunza is a safe haven. No one takes advantage of anyone's property so if you think you can walk into any orchard and devour the juicy treats, you cannot. You sincerely should not.

We actually entered someone's private fruit garden, as we went for an evening stroll around our guesthouse. Unaware, for we had no clue but there was nobody we could apologize to.

The tourist heaven Hunza Valley is the central piece of Karakorum. Hunza Karimabad is the only town, where you can view the five famous peaks Rakaposhi 7788m, Golden peak 7027m Diran 7256m Ultar I 7388m, Ultar II 7310m and Ladyfinger peak, to name a few. Ladyfinger turned out to be the most exceptional peaks of all in the valley and my son's favourite.

We were walking up a winding cobblestone path in Karimabad towards Baltit Fort which was closed at the time. So we mutually agreed to explore the marketplace. Karimabad is full of handicrafts, wood arts, mountaineering equipment, gemstones, dry fruits, herbs, fresh fruits and small hotels until u reach the Baltit Fort. You will be tempted to try on some vibrant hand embroidered caps, laced with semi-precious stones jewelry and other embellishments and purchase a variety of dry fruits. Hunzakuts are known to hold great pride in their traditional caps; each one has a different story. So I bought a typical one for my kid, which I have always admired. Minus the feather for that is an expensive feather, which they proudly adorn in their warm caps.

We returned from our excursion back to our guest house in about 3 hours. Slept like a log until morning, right after dinner, followed by a long chit-chat under the apricot tree.

* **Tip:** Dry Shampoo is always a convenient option. Not the best but reasonably convenient.

Day 03 – The Excitement Continues
11th July 2016

Plan: Breakfast then drive to Attabad Lake via Attabad tunnel, free time for photography & drive to Khunjerab Pass via Passu & Sost valley.
Enjoy the drive via KKH & amazing view of the snowcapped Mountains around. Explore Khunjerab Pass (Pak-China border) & return back to Passu for dinner & overnight camping

Prior to this trip my son and I have never gone camping nor have we ever seen a border except in the movies and documentaries. Therefore, this day had a different feel of excitement for me and Rayyan.

The Hunza morning at Café de Pamir was marvelous. The sun lights up Rakaposhi's summit as I stretch my arms at half past 6 in the morning, breathing in the clean fresh air. Rakaposhi Mountain is undoubtedly the valley's most well-known peak. The huge range dominates the skyline for a vast stretch of the Karakoram highway. I feel fortunate to be able to enjoy one of the most stunning views on earth. And Climax Adventure Pakistan always makes sure that your place to stay has the perfect views of the valley.

Right after our usual omelette, paratha and tea breakfast had a dozen ripe succulent apricots we were to set off for another expedition. You just cannot have enough of this luscious treat. My fantasy to have fruit picked from the tree finally came true and with permission this time, from the most humble Karim Khan sahab owner of the Café and Amin, their pizza expert. Sitting under the shade of trees, enjoying the faint sweet smell of apricots, cracking open the pit to eat the seed - the joys of being in the mountains away from the chaotic city life! We decided to click a few pictures on the terrace not letting go of the opportunity to miss the magnificent blue sky and majestic Rakaposhi covered with snow in the background. On the way up I spotted a walnut tree, a hard green fruit, earlier I never anticipated how walnuts grow. The roof of the café was covered with solar panels, this was the first time I saw it here in Hunza. Little did I know it was a quite a norm in Gilgit.

"There are around 200 houses in Shimshal and every house uses solar panels to generate electricity," a proud local Shambi Khan says. He proudly adds that compared to other people living at a similar altitude — 3,000 meters above sea level in Asia — Shimshal's residents enjoy a much better quality of life. Shimshal is nestled deep in Hunza Valley, sharing a border with China's Xinjiang region. Shimshal is the largest village of Hunza valley. Its extensive pasture lands include; Shimshal Pamir, Gujerav, Yazghail and Loopghar. The Shimshal Pamir Lake attracts many tourists to it.

Ghulam Shah — a social activist and tourist guide acknowledged the fact that solar panels are good to light houses, but cannot be used to run heavy electrical items.

Today was a long day; I was looking forward to travel from Aliabad to Khunjerab Pass.

Karakoram Highway – The world's best road trip

We were to start our journey from Aliabad, cross Karimabad, Attabad, Gulmit, Hussaini, Passu, Jamalabad, Sost, all the way to Khunjerab, along Hunza River. The river cuts through the Karakoram and flows over at length along the constructed highway.

The Karakoram Highway often just called KKH is a highway that runs about 1.300km (800 miles) from

Abbottabad in Pakistan to Kashgar in the province of Xinjiang in West China. Today the border crossing between Pakistan and China is on Khunjerab Pass at 4800m (16.00feet), officially the world's highest border crossing. It begins from Havelian and coils through many scenic spots such as Mansehra, Thakot, Abbottabad, Besham, Pattan, Sazin, Chilas, Gilgit Baltistan and Hunza, connecting China's Xinjiang region with Pakistan's Gilgit–Baltistan region in Khyber Pakhtunkhwa at an altitude of 4,693 m/15,397 ft.

Indeed it is the technique of modern engineering which carved this colossal roadway in such a grueling area — about 15,000 men of the Pakistan Army along with Chinese workers came together to cut through one of the most challenging terrains in the world. The fearless road builders of China and Pakistan took almost 20 years to complete this 805-mile long highway which has been stretched over the hills, gorges, valleys and rivers.

Unfortunately one fateful day a huge mountain fell over the KKH and blocked the water of the Hunza River to become a lake at Attabad, Hunza Valley of Gilgit-Baltistan. Hence, the trade between China and Pakistan had virtually come to a standstill. China and Pakistan together reconnected the flooded portion of the KKH in the Attabad Lake by constructing five tunnels, two bridges and 78 channels. The road is now open to all types of traffic between China and Pakistan. The tunnels, named as the Pakistan-China Friendship Tunnels now open the 24 kilometers stretch of the KKH damaged since the 2010 massive landslides.

The first tunnel – the Attabad tunnel led us to the bluest of lakes – the Attabad Lake, near Gojal valley. A little more than half an hour we reached Passu, with a welcome note right under the Passu cones which said, 'WELCOME TO PASSU'. We got off for a little stretch, a little photography at this small village on the Karakoram Highway, besides the Hunza River. Tupopdan (20,033 ft), also known as "Passu Cones" or "Passu Cathedral", lies to the north of the Passu village; it is the most photographed peak of the Passu region. The people are Wakhi and speak the Wakhi Language.

Although it was a bright sunny morning the gushing river makes it up for the weather. At this point I was unaware that we will be camping here for the night. This place had some pretty wild flowers. Lavender stood out amongst all in the same wildflower patch with pretty yellow collections of tiny blossoms all clustered together.

From Passu we moved towards Sost, which took an hour long drive through the gorgeous mountains. I distinctly remember where we stopped for a washroom break at main market Sost. Outside was a sign: Four Brothers Hotel and Corridor Restaurant.

Sost is a beautiful village on edge of Pakistan-China Border where thousands of tourists come to explore its mightiness. This border is the initial trade point where trade facilitation center is located; trucks from china dump their goods at this place. Sost is the last point of Hunza Valley.

After 15 minutes of drive towards Khunjerab Pass we stopped at a Wildlife check post. A sign that said: **Natural Environment and Wildlife are our Future** – was completely violated. To my dismay there was a snow leopard cub in a very miserable state. Left listlessly in a small brick shack, caged, away from the jungle, under the scorching July sun.

Hut-bound baby snow leopard

All hell broke loose when the little cub and his mother were crossing a river near the Khunjerab National Park in Gilgit Baltistan in late December. In a sorry turn of fate, the leopardess reached the other side, but her child, who had hurt himself, was left behind. Upon being spotted by guards of the wildlife department, the little ball of fur was brought to a small village on the Pak-China border called Dhee and labeled Qiq Maman, which means 'little boy' in the local Wakhi language. Visibly 'forest-sick', Qiq Maman lazes away on his mat in the hut, and looks quite uncared for. The hut is both stuffy and dusty as the wildlife department fails to abide by the standard of allowing animals a replica of their natural habitat in captivity – a problem stemming / surfacing largely due to lack of funds. Much to my relief I recently found out the wild mammal is in a better place now!

Back on track, heading straight to Khunjerab Pass. The luxury of planning a trip with an experienced Adventure tour group is you do not have to worry about check posts, entry fees, proving your identity etc.

While this was being taken care of we got off to explore the place where there was a famous Khunjerab National Park of Gilgit Baltistan where there was camping facility in designated areas. The place had an extraordinary serenity to it. On the way we could see golden marmots and it's not easy clicking them from a moving vehicle. We also came across 3 indolent but sociable Yaks who patiently let us ride and pose with them.

* **Tip:** Keep something warm to drink in a flask and an extra pair of socks. It will be revealed shortly, why that is essential.

The highest border in the world and an incredible accomplishment of human engineering, the road to the Pakistani-Chinese border is full of stunning peaks and makes for a great day trip. Approximately in half an hour the Pak-China border was visible. It was 3 pm but the temperature had dropped and we had to layer up before we advanced further.

The Khunjerab Pass is the world's highest international border at 4800m (16.00feet), this being the highest point at Karakoram peak. It is so intriguing that the first glimpse of its charms you. The completion of the section of this road was done in 1982. It is said to be the highest border crossing on Earth. The border closes down 1st of December to around 1st of May every year (that may be conditional due to unpredictable weather changes)

A mass of people had gathered around the border, clicking pictures, filming, group photographs and the growing trend of selfies. You will find a 'Tribute to the Pioneers' wall. You can see snow covered mountains on both side of the borders. It is here where we took our first group snapshot. By this time we were all bonding fairly well. Dodging a cluster of white, yellow and purple attractive wild flowers (*primulas – I assume*) we took off for a meaningless walk. We reached a slab of ice with the melted water flowing in what seemed like a stream. We scraped the ice from the glacier and had a little snow / ice fight. Our hands were not prepared for this. Here something strange happened. Our cell phone clocks automatically adjusted to a different time zone (3 hours ahead) which left us thinking daylight at quarter to 8?!!

*** Tip:** Always follow the guide if there is one. You may wander off having little or no clue of a strange land. Your intelligence may mislead you and you will end up taking a longer route, with no easy way out.

In order to find our path back to our ride we got lost in the maze. As luck would have it Rasheed bhai (our guide) found us wandering and lost. There was only one alternative to go across – to take a big leap, as far as the legs would stretch. Out of four of us only Taiba was able to cross the stream flawlessly. The rest including me were drenched in icy cold water. That's when an extra pair of socks and warm delicious Lahori – doodhpatti (tea from Lahore) came to the rescue.

Unexpectedly one of our group members bumped into a friend who offered the tea. The finest I have had so far with just the right amount of milk and sugar.

It was almost dark when we reached Passu. We checked-in **Glacier Breeze Café and Restaurant**, a restaurant perched on the glacier moraine overlooking Passu village and KKH. The superb location has the glacier stream rushing beside it with 360 panoramic view including Passu Glacier, Passu Cathedrals. Another great option is the **Passu Tourist Lodge** - which is one of the popular hotels located in Passu, Gojal, Hunza. We camped at Glacier Breeze Café. Personally I was intimidated by the camp site, the nightfall, Hunza River crashing around large river rocks and a cloudy moonlit night. Unaware until this moment that Passu provides comfortable and safe camping site for tourists, we dropped our baggage outside the restaurant, waiting to be served. The aroma of the famous apricot cake fills the air which makes the almost 120 steps worth climbing.

Hunza River meets with Nagar River and other regional rivers on its course down to the south. It eventually adds up into the mighty Indus.

This place had a decent washroom and the sound of the river was delightful, something we treasured.

After dinner my friend and I decided to just lie on the uneven concrete and gaze at the stars twinkling brightly in the moonlit sky, playing hide and seek with thick clouds. We ordered a mug of coffee and the chef served the yummiest coffee as promised. So far I have met the most cultured and humble people, which makes the trip all the more worthwhile. Glacier Breeze café has the world famous Apricot cake a specialty of the region baked by Chef Ahmet. Baked simply, the cake was fresh, warm and syrupy, served with the most aromatic special green tea (tumoro) and perfectly brewed French Press coffee.

As we rest comfortably on the ground, I spotted a falling star! The night was an experience in itself. Surrounded by these legendary peaks, into the wild, river full of life, curving around giant round rocks, with over a dozen colourful camps on one side, the moon taking cover behind the thick clouds, stars glistening in the sky, brimming mug of coffee, temperature dropping, and the idea of snuggling in a camp outdoors.

Here is where we needed our emergency lights the most. The cozy camp with an inviting sleeping bag put me into deep sleep.

* **Tip:** Keep your emergency lights / cell phone charged before it gets dark. Due to power failures in the Northern areas it can get really difficult. Here is where your power banks / extra batteries come to the rescue.

The village of Passu is located among the towering peaks of the Karakoram Mountain Range. A peaceful retreat in the very heart of magnificent mountain scenery: Pointed unclimbed and un-scale able rock peaks, ice-demes with sharp fluted ridges; stand like knife blades. The village is surrounded by a huge wall of mountains and is the base of three important valleys: Shimshal, Khunjerab and Batura, as well as the short valley of the Passu Glacier.

On the way to Shimshal and Pamir, there are 9 glaciers. Each glacier represents a medium trek of 7 or more days. From the glaciers flow streams which empty into the Shimshal River. The Khunjerab stream is fed along the bay by the Mintaka Misgar and Yeshkok Chipursan streams which become the Khunjerab River.

From the 40 miles long Batura Glacier the water flows with such intensity that the Batura River has once damaged the R.C.C. Bridge in Karakoram highway (KKH). These three rivers from the three large valleys join at Passu, therefore, making Passu the water shed of the three incredible valleys.

Day 4 – The Hiking Day 12th July 2016

Plan: Breakfast & drive to Hussaini valley. Hike up to Borith Lake (30mins), explore Borith Lake. Hike up to Passu glacier (3hrs), Explore Passu glacier & amazing view of Karakoram mountains including Passu peak-7478m, Shispare Peak-7611m & more. Hike back to Hussiani valley, Explore Hussaini Suspension bridge. Drive to Ghulkin valley, explore the valley. Bus ride & drive back to Hunza for dinner & overnight stay.

If you wish to see a beautiful sunrise over Gulmit or Passu cathedrals you have to wake up pretty early. The arches on the mountains make a setting for a beautiful and colorful show, with sun's rays hitting the ridge at an angle resulting in a panoramic dance of light and shadows observed on the mountain ranges. It was quarter past 4 when I woke up to see the first light over the mountaintop. You have to be there to experience the grand spectacle. It takes time for one to take the landscape in, the rugged mountains, and rock-strewn path leading down to the Hunza River, the prickly wild plants, apple trees and pretty lavender. The apples were not quite ready yet. It is the perfect place for taking panoramic photos of the Passu cones. If you do not do that, you will probably regret it until you take the next trip.

Perhaps this was the first time nearly everyone woke up before Rasheed bhai had a chance to wake us up. The staple omelet, paratha breakfast welcomed us. I ordered the coffee again after my last night's experience. At the breakfast table a bunch of us had a nice warm discussion about a lot of things, history, places, events, travelling, and gender issues. I loved the group members I was travelling with. It was a blessing to have such wonderful people on board. Immediately after breakfast we had to pack and be back on the road. It started drizzling which did not last long, but gave a pleasant start to our journey. We clicked a few pictures on the roadside with lavender blossoming on one side and the river flowing on either side. The large Hunza River flows aggressively through one of the prettiest places on Earth. A small road separates the main highway and mounts over a ridge to Borith Lake. Basically, Passu is one of the bases and onset point for trekkers heading towards the different valleys.

Leaving behind the deep valley for a little oasis tucked in between two glaciers. On one side there is Passu Glacier, which comes flowing out of the mountain tops and melts into a small lake above the village of Passu. The road ends at the bottom of the glacier on a steep drop off with insane views. A trail leads up the moraine ridge on a skinny track along a rock wall.

It took us barely 20 minutes to reach Borith Lake from Passu. The very instant we reached, our hike began. I was oblivious to the fact that my legs are strong enough to help me climb mountains. The inspiration was the lake itself. I did not Google any of these places earlier so there were many surprises particularly for me on this journey. The hike was a little more than half an hour before we caught a glimpse of the translucent lake between the tall trees. Climb down the stepping stones to reach the edge of the lake. The serenity, the tranquility, the clear sparkling water, the dragonflies and the vibrant butterflies was something I can go back to again and again. We enjoyed chasing the orange and blue dragonflies around the wild bushes and trees surrounded by gorgeous wild yellow flowers.

Borith Lake – Beauty beyond words
Borith lake Uper Hunza, Gojal, with the reflection of Ultar Mountain, was once a popular hunting place

for the Mir of Hunza during winters, particularly for birds. A small house was built for the Mir on a hill surrounding the lake just on the edge. Today this house is known as the Borith Lake Hotel. Today the lake has reduced in size, salty over the years due to a reduction in the underground seepage that feeds it. This is the result of receding glaciers and an impact of climatic changes.

The lake is a magnificent bird sanctuary for migrating wildfowl or waterfowls – ducks, geese and swans etc. that stay here on their journey towards the cold regions of Central Asia. This marveling wonder becomes so attractive in the months of March and June when many species of waterfowls arrive from the warmer regions of the Southern Pakistan. A hotel here Borith Lake Hotel is run by Mr. Tawakal Khan. A nice and polite person, retired army man who is always very friendly and smiling and enjoys dancing!

This lake is rather unusual. The water is not exactly brine (saltwater), but leaves a white crust on your skin once it is dry. It has an unusual taste similar to sulfur or high in alkaline. Obviously I did not taste it. The locals call it a soda lake. Naturally there were not any fish because they are unable to survive in this water.

Borith Lake – a complete break from everything; from the Internet, television, phones, the urge to share pictures with family, honking cars and traffic, city pollution, the noise and the furor. An absolute change of pace; basically this entire trip was. Along the Borith Lake Hotel there are some grassy areas overlooking the lake to set up camps. What a beautiful sight it would be to wake up to every morning. Around 6 or 7 a.m the reflection of the mountains is at its best. If there is not a breath of wind the lake is like a giant mirror. I wish we had camped here too.

The infamous *chacha* (uncle) Tawakkal Khan, who became prominent after the Humans of New York gentleman, the street photographer Brandon Stanton, visited this place and interviewed him. You will meet him when you visit Borith Lake Hotel and Restaurant where you can dine and stay. Some say videos of him dancing are viral in Japan too. He enjoys doing that for his guests. Both make the hike up to the lake worthwhile, Mr. Tawakal Khan and the Borith Lake. It is very common for trekkers and visitors to stay at the lake overnight and witness the glorifying break of dawn. Lakes are at their best in the morning if you wish to see mirror-image. The lake has assorted books available for purchase as well. An interesting book that I got my hands on was titled; 'Let's Go to My Favorite Travel Country, Let's Go to Pakistan – By Gilbert Kolonko. You will find this book here only but I was told a handful of them are left now.

A relatively longer trekking route can be taken if you like to visit the Passu Gar Glacier by continuing the journey south ways from Borith Lake. The Passu Glacier is one of the white glaciers in Hunza valley. Many tourists visit it every year.

*** Tip:** Before you set off for your hike towards the Glaciers request the people at the hotel for the book you need. So they have ample time to arrange until you return.

While looking around the hotel I saw Tawakkal *chacha* (uncle) has very proudly put up a print out of HONYs Face book page, amongst other pictures of the Passu and Gulkhin glaciers, suspension bridges and Borith Sir. We spent almost an hour at the lush green surroundings of the emerald green lake, exploring the lakes, taking group photos before we hiked up the rugged terrain we had to travel through to get to the glacier – my very first glacier.

I had never anticipated what was to come. Even the fittest of us could not hike up effortlessly. It took us one and a half hour to get a glimpse of something white – pure white. It took us another half an hour to reach the top. When we set off at 9 it was not exactly sunny. When we reached the mountain top it was sweltering hot. Imagine the sight – sun shining with all its might, legs hurting, a quite deserted place. This was my very first trekking experience and I was glad there was a guide with us. Each member of our group started at their own pace, chit chatting, grumbling yet moving forward, with Rasheed bhai's encouraging words that we can do it, just a little more, only a little way up. High mountains, clear trek, green meadows on one side, wild fruit trees, occasional resident in the best looking valley, steep and rocky pathway. I was especially awe struck by the incredulous oversized pieces of rocks on one side of the trek. In the middle of the deserted mountain crest you may spot a lizard instantly camouflaging itself to avoid danger. It was strange to see tadpoles growing in a long duct along the mountain walls.

*** Tip:** Carry sunscreen and a water bottle with you, to keep yourself protected and hydrated, especially if you are trekking during summers at sunlight hours. Keep your trail mix with you to keep yourself energized. You may not come across a waterfall, but when you reach your destination you will be able to enjoy pure glacier water.

We assumed it would be cold up there but fatefully it was not. Nonetheless we had the pleasure to enjoy chilled glacier water on a sizzling day. All praises to our fearless guide who hiked down with a bag full of plastic bottles to fill them with some fresh glacial water. Glacial ice is the largest reservoir of fresh water on Earth. The hike back was really good and we got so carried away talking that we lost our way. And at that very moment we were grateful to have a tour guide around who again found us, two wandering souls. Our legs could not carry us, any longer as we reached the comforting lake and that's when we met the famous *chacha* (uncle) Tawaakal Khan. Such a friendly positive spirit he is. We also met his sons who help him run the place. You may never encounter this extent of modesty and hospitality in the metropolitan areas of Pakistan. It occurred to me that our group members rowed their way back to the hotel, while my friend and I got off tracked and sunburned. They all had a good laugh especially when I began complaining and fuming - all in good humour!

One of our group members decided to stay back and be the chef for the day. And I am glad she did. She served us delicious rice and special yogurt potatoes. Dead on our feet we quietly wolfed down the food whilst commending her on her culinary skills. Imagine they let an outsider cook in their kitchen!

By mid-afternoon we hiked back down to drive to Hussaini Suspension Bridge. I did not have any energy to march down the bridge. So I relaxed in the coaster, while chit-chatting with a few worn out members. But I decided to cross the Hussaini Bridge one day... and I did! A year after this trip had the opportunity to go back. Walking on the death bridge is an experience in itself. The pleasure you get once you reach the end – the view, the river beneath, the scary hanging bridge and the silver- gold speckled rock formations! You must dare to cross it at least once in your lifetime. I am glad I did!

As we drove down, we left behind the last green village set into the brown landscape. Then nothing but rock, river, and bright blue sky fill your vision. You zigzag up one side of the gigantic slide and over the top to the tropical blue waters of Attabad Lake. It instantly brightens your mood.

Attabad – the Sapphire of the North

In between the rugged peaks of Hunza rests the Attabad Lake also known as Gojal Lake which was formed in the year 2010, as a consequence of a massive land sliding at Attabad village in Gojal valley, Gilgit Baltistan. This is Pakistan's biggest artificial lake in Hunza valley, Gilgit Baltistan. In 2010 a huge landslide happened at the village of Attabad, which blocked the Hunza River and ended up creating a 22 km lake. A large section of the Karakoram Highway ended up underwater along with parts of Shishkat, Ainabad, Gulmit, and Husaini villages. Eventually a massive cut was made through the slide and water began flowing. The lake is smaller than what it once grew to in size, but it's still huge. There were debates in the beginning whether to drain or not to drain the lake or just build the road or tunnel above it. Hence, the decision was taken to make a tunnel. The sparkling blue lake... the bluest lake I have ever seen, connects the glorious Hunza valley and the Passu area.

A series of well-made tunnels will take you to the Attabad Lake where the old clunky colorful wooden boats wait to ferry passengers to the other end or back, sometimes big and small vehicles.

We spent an hour here, as we watched the glistening sunshine over the enormous peaks and onto the sparkling still water where the only ripples created are because of the boats. In the distance you can see colossal Passu peaks hiding behind the clouds. Taking a moment to soak in the landscape, where we all did our fair share of modeling and photography!

The road is clear and lake is reachable throughout the year through the local transport in no time from Aliabad and Karimabad as well. On our way out, there was a bundle of raw wool sitting on a stone with two legs sticking out. Turned out it was a lambskin perched on a large rock. It took us an hour to reach back home – Hunza our home away from home. Karim bhai the owner of Café de Pamir was kind enough to drive us to the Karimabad bakery. While he made his purchase for our dinner that night, I started hunting for the big, plump and rich in flavor Hunza cherries. I stumbled upon some oversized vegetables – eggplant cucumbers and the roundest carrots.

Way past the midnight, I decided to wash clothes, with the unpleasantly cold glacier water. Everything here was different, even the way you wash clothes, and I wanted to add that to the many quirky adventures I have had. The idea of attempting something I never dreamt of, never thought of is always actually tempting. There was a large dull metal dish (*thaal*) and it was good fun to wash my clothes in it and hung it on the clothesline to dry until morning.

*** Tip:** Always make sure to check if the tap water you are using is glacial water, before washing clothes or taking a shower. Although it is clean water but it leaves traces of earth.
Reminder to self: That should not be a problem!

Day 05 – Hunza as I see it 13th July 2016

Plan: *Break Fast and drive to Hopper valley Nagar (1:30hrs), Hike up to Hopper Glacier (1hr), enjoy the glacier view & all high mountains around, hike down & drive back to Hunza Karimabad for lunch, drive to Duikar for sunset and better view of all the high mountains & the valley, Enjoy breathtaking view of Karakoram Mountains on the trek, Rakaposhi-7785m, Diran Peak-7200m, Spantik/Golden Peak-7027m, Ultar Peak-7344m and the hopper glacier. Drive back to Hotel for dinner & overnight stay.*

Hunza Valley is situated at an elevation of 2,438 meters. The tourist season is from May to October. The temperature in May is maximum 27°C and minimum 14°C. The October temperatures are: maximum 10°C and minimum 0°C. The local languages spoken in Gilgit include Burushaski, Wakhi, Shina, Balti and Khowar/Chitrali. Urdu and English are also understood by most of the people 95% Urdu and 75% English. Urdu is the national language and is spoken throughout Pakistan as lingua franca – the language bridge. As elsewhere in Pakistan, English is fairly widely spoken among the educated classes and those involved in the tourist industry.

Linguistic Treasures of Gilgit Baltistan

The **Shina** language (with several dialects like Asturjaa, Kharuchaa, Chilasi) is the language of 60% of the population, spoken mainly in Gilgit, Astore throughout Diamer, and in some parts of Ghizer. The **Balti dialect**, a sub-dialect of Ladakhi and part of the Tibetan languages group, is spoken by the entire population of Baltistan.

Minor languages spoken in the region include **Wakhi**, spoken in upper Hunza, and in some villages in Ghizer, while Khowar is the language of Ghizer. **Burushaski** is an isolated language spoken in Hunza, Nagar, Yasin (where Khowar is also spoken), in some parts of Gilgit and in some villages of Punyal.

Another interesting language is **Domaaki**, spoken by the musician clans in the region. A small minority of people also speak Pashto. Despite being referred to as part of **Kashmir**, Gilgit-Baltistan has few remnants of Kashmiri speaking their own language. *(Taken from various sources over the Internet)*

The literacy rate of the Hunza valley is believed to be more than 90%. Virtually every child is educated up to at least high school level. The lifestyle of Hunzakuts is very simple. Most of the inhabitants of Hunza are Ismaili Muslims, followers of Prince Karim Aga Khan IV, while in Ganish more than 65% are Twelver Shia Muslims. Hunza region is principally home to people of four ethnicities:

The Lower Hunza area - from Khizerabad to Nasirabad is mainly inhabited by the Shinaki people who are Shina speakers.

The Central Hunza area - from Murtazaabad to Attabad is mainly inhabited by Burushaski speakers, however, there is a centuries-old locally inhabiting community as well that is known as the 'Domaki' which lives in a village lying in the immediate vicinity of 'Baltit' called 'Mominabad'.

The Upper Hunza area, known as Gojal - from Shishkat to Khunjerab is mainly populated by Wakhi speakers from a Central Asian origin while Burushaski speakers have recently being settled by Mir Nazim Khan.

Hunzakuts drink substantial amounts of "Glacial Milk" which is milky coloured fresh water melted from the base of glaciers, rich in rock flour and minerals. Therefore, we avoided taking a bath in Hunza. You really have to compromise on your luxurious bathroom needs. And as I mentioned earlier you end up making peace with it, presumably because you have so much fun stuff to be excited about. Especially the Hunza morning as the colossal snow-capped Rakaposhi glows in the morning light. What a sight it was. No camera can capture the glory of the giant peak glowing under the sunrays. It is while I was compiling my book that I came across the secret to *Hunzakuts* gorgeous skin;

Hunzakuts only drink and bathe in the pure glacier water that comes directly from the mountains. Their most famous 'not-so-secret' drink is an herbal tea that is made from boiled glacier water and a herb known as Tumoro. This herbal tea is made from wild thyme, an interesting tea for non-Hunza, most of who do not think of thyme as an herb used in tea! Valued for its medicinal properties it is said to alleviate headaches, calm nerves and soothe sore throats. The glacier water and herbs are the reason they have such glowing skin.

On the contrary, we outwardly cosmopolitan people reckon the glacier water is safe to drink not fit for bathing. Some of us still believe it is soiled and should not be consumed. But if you are not troubled by the idea drink away! For an hour clicked pictures around until breakfast was served. You just cannot capture Hunza on the lens enough. At that very moment I realized I cannot capture the magnificence of this landscape, the feeling of peace and the gorgeous silhouettes of the mountains. I can only capture a piece of time with my camera. With every photo that I click I remember the day, the time, the scene, the place and that thought which makes me press the shutter more than once. Certain things cannot be seized such as your experiences or the lessons learned during your journey.

Clouds scattered in the blue sky, birds chirping, Rakaposhi standing with all its might, radiant under the morning sunlight. For the first time today I caught sight of a **black billed magpie** – a stunning bird, flying through the soaring Himalayan silver fir and the poplar trees swaying under the breeze. No photograph that I have taken has ever captured how much I love it, how much I need it and how much I will miss it. Photographs are mere memories full of variety of emotions which cannot be described in words.

*** Tip:** Moments like these are still worth capturing so make videos of stuff you like watching repeatedly, which will stir you back to the wonderful time you once had.

It was our second breakfast in Hunza under the walnut tree. Omelette, paratha, doodh-patti (milk tea) and two different kinds of jams was the everyday breakfast. We had already explored parts of Upper-Hunza Valley; today was a day to travel around Central Hunza and Hunza's highest village Duikar.

At about 2800m, Duikar is about 11km which is approximately 25 minutes' drive from Karimabad, past gravity-defying terraced fields. As you reach the top, the reward awaits you – immense valley views. From the mysteriously eroded hill behind Eagle's Nest Hotel you can look down on the Hunza River, the KKH and the Altit village; or look across to Rakaposhi and Golden Peak (Diran Peak is hidden); and up to the Ladyfinger Peak. Sunrise and sunsets are magnificent here.

The previous night we had spoken to our guide and expressed our interest in staying behind and hanging around Aliabad and Karimabad. We did not have a concrete plan chalked out but the intention was to interact with the locals, become acquainted with the marketplace, learn about the culture, form relationship with people we did not know and see what a day in Hunza is really like. Somehow the group planned to leave late. So my friend and I decided to get dressed and wander around. Our plan for the day was to meet the locals and perhaps witness how they live. Five minutes outside our guesthouse on a clean deserted stone-wall road we met this middle-aged man dressed interestingly; a belt around his shirt (*kurta*), mid-calf boots, shovel in hand and the typical pleasant Hunza smile. He could not speak or understand Urdu so we used sign language to communicate and agreed to get a picture taken with my son.

I loved the spotless street, with the tall trees towering above us, awesome cloudy weather and the gentle wind blowing. While roving aimlessly we noticed a native woman washing a rather large dish, with a warm smile welcoming us. Her name was Gul-e-Shireen and in a glance you know how well she carried her name. She invited us in and disappeared herself. Little did we know the steps we ascended will take us to an Inspector *sahab's* family! Gul-e-Shireen was his older brother's wife who lived downstairs. I am not quite sure if it was his apricot orchard we trespassed 3 days back.

Well, this was just the beginning to what was in store for us. It was a little awkward for the less hospitable Karachittes that we were raised as. The Inspector sahib and his family were so warm and welcoming, they offered us fresh off the tree red mouthwatering cherries. There was no way I could decline the offer. His son who was also a Police officer himself climbed up the ladder to gather them. Hunzakuts take pride in growing their own plantations. Apart from their cherished gold trees (apricots) they cultivate other fruits and vegetables, some even go to the extent of growing mountain herbs in their gardens. The family we visited seemed to have had everything, from pretty roses and delicate flowers to underground carrots, potatoes and onions, alongside cherries and two different kinds of apples.

After introducing himself he delightfully told us he got married in the year 1981 and has 3 daughters and a son. "Eldest is a Masters in Economics and working as a teacher. My second one is also a teacher and third one is doing her MBA. My son is like me working as a Police officer. He is married and has a daughter," he spoke with great pride.

The little baby Inaya seemed to be the apple of the eye of not only the grandparents but the entire household. He further told us he has lived and worked in different parts of Karachi for almost 8 years.

Each individual you come across in this Valley has very strong sense of trust and loyalty towards their community – where everyone is a relative, a neighbour, a brother. He sincerely feels Hunza has been ignored and neglected by the Government and is all praises for Prince Karim Agha Khan who has genuinely worked for the Hunzakuts in terms of education, health, construction and developmental work. But as he spoke, he was also optimistic that Hunza will progress with the "KKH route recently renovated and Chinese CPEC projects, Chinese investors and Chinese Government's recent unannounced projects in the pipeline."

Each individual you come across in this part of the world will proudly testify that their literacy rate is a 100%. And they have the right to flaunt it. Before leaving his serene abode we learnt the Burushaski language *une gueek besan bila ?* (What is your name?) "*Weekh ehsen dilaa*" 20 minutes and a couple of group pictures later we left for our dearly loved café cum home. It is here that I realized how much I wish to get to know these unpretentious and humble people and their lifestyles.

Hunza Homes

The *Hunzakuts* cut the foundation into the bed of rock, to provide a secure footing for his home against landslides and earthquakes. They keep the walls low and make the windows and doors small and few in number, to keep out the cold winter winds and to further stabilize the structure. They embed wooden posts within the masonry to provide support for the roof, as protection in case the masonry walls were to collapse in this seismic region. The home could be built with mud but a house built of stone will last for a hundred years. The **Baltit fort** was built on a base of heavy stones without mortar, so that the basis could shift and settle rather than crumple once the ground began to move. Horizontal wooden beams were laid on either side of the walls to provide a flexible structure to hold the masonry in place and prevent collapse. At the corners, these overlapping beams created a space which formed a continuous column which when filled with rubble stone further strengthens these points of greatest weakness. Consequently this creates an effective indigenous structural system which is developed throughout the Karakoram and Himalayan region.

Many homes in Hunza today have retained or reproduced the traditional scheme with four posts, defining the square inner space of the dwelling. A number of old houses in Hunza and Nagar still preserve the more ancient form of posts with two step-like transitions to the capital (similar to Baltit Fort). You will notice variations in the form and decoration of the base and of the adjoining bulbous, often fluted part. The different levels of working, resting, sitting, and sleeping platforms around the common space of a traditional house are sometimes bordered by low railings decorated with floral patterns. The central roof opening above the space, composed of an overlay of decreasing, diagonally superimposed squares of small beams, constitutes an essential carpentry task and marks, structurally and symbolically, which is the navel of the house and the place of the fireplace.

Back from our brief expedition, the group bundled up in the coaster and reached Karimabad. As planned we fanned out in different directions, and mutually decided to meet for lunch. First stop in the market place was **Hunza Wood Art** which had an amazing craftsmanship display of all kinds of spoons. Mulberry, apricot, cherry, birch, walnut, pear trees, etc. were proudly hanging in all shapes sizes and designs; each had its own distinct smell. Everything was handcrafted in the little workshop in the corner of the shop. Spent a good 20 minutes photographing, admiring, and making a good purchase of the fine handiwork, left the shop promising to visit the place again. Five minutes of walking around came across a gem shop, to find one of the most humble, hospitable and generous shop owners. After buying rings and earrings and chit chatting with this gentleman, found out what the Hunzakuts really desire. In his own words, we are all very settled in our businesses, thanks to our forefathers. We are not greedy for money. We just want enough to educate our children, their education is our priority and that's what we earn and live for!

Talking to this very interesting gentleman who gave Rayyan 2 semi-precious stones in its raw form as a souvenir and did not want us to feel left out so gave us a necklace each, saying we honour our guests. You actually have to meet these people to see how incredible they are, with their extraordinary warmth and kindness. Almost everyone in the Karimabad offered us water; tea or drink and some went to the extent to offer lunch. Strolling around, we visited many little shops with fresh, genuine honey, jams and dried fruits to all sorts of handicrafts. You will also come across many hand embroidered items, all sorts of traditional caps and handicrafts, carpets, art galleries, dry fruit places, mountaineering equipment which you can buy, sell or rent, restaurants who delightfully serve local delicacies and hotels to eat and to stay.

One shop which differed from others, North Gems and Hanicrafts owned by Amir Khan sahab, had an entire wall of books, travel guides, maps etc. It's unlikely for me not to purchase a book on a trip. Sure enough I picked a book – **Hunza Lost Kingdom of Himalayas** – an interesting read. In like 15 minutes this guy who wasn't the sole owner, passionately started talking about Hunza's history, Baltit Fort and the Altit Fort.

"Hunza has been ruled by the family known as Mirs of Hunza for 960 years. The Hunzakuts are believed to be the descendents of five wandering soldiers of Alexander the Great. Here we mainly speak Brushuski language. This princely state retained its isolated independence for a long time in the remote part of the areas. During early nineteenth century, Hunza resented Kashmir's attempts to gain control and its rulers periodically expelled Kashmir battalions, threatened Gilgit, and politicked with the rulers of Kashgar to the north where the Russians were gaining influence. Fearing Russians infiltration into their northern frontiers, the British took over direct political control at Gilgit in 1889. This, coupled with the Mir of Hunza's consistent intransigence induced the British to march on Hunza in December 1891,

*where they fought a decisive battle at Nilit, 60 km
beyond Diaynor Bridge. After this the British occupied
force in Aliabad until 1897 when Hit became a
princely state protected by the Government of British
India. After Pakistan was created in 1947, the people
of Hunza also gained liberation and the princely state
was merged in Pakistan."*

Short of cash, we were waiting for the power to
return to Karimabad, and this gentleman offered us
cash to visit the forts. Being hardcore Karachittes we
were not ready for this generous proposal. Complete
strangers to him, he was not ready to take no for an
answer, we in turn left some of our belongings with
him, against his wishes. He insisted not to leave
Hunza until we have seen the Forts, even if you skip
one. His strong recommendation was the Baltit Fort.

Baltit Fort is a kilometer away from Karimabad.
It was built 700 years ago by 30 labourers brought to
Hunza in the dowry of the Princess of Baltistan when
she married Mir of Hunza. The area is named Baltit
after those labourers. Over the centuries it has been
inhabited by the ruling family of the Hunza State.
The Fort is a wood-and-stone structure with mud
plaster. It is a three story building, with granaries
and some stores in the basement on a glacier
moraine hill with man-made narrow terraces for the
stability of its ancient foundations.

I especially loved the second floor which features
an impressive open terrace with a royal throne under
a beautiful Mogul style wooden canopy, living rooms,
bay windows with balcony and breath-taking views.
The fort is an experience in itself. *Salahuddin bhai,*
the guard outside the fort, stands proudly with his
extraordinary prominent mustache, a pleasant man,
always ready to pose for you. I admired how ardently
he told someone, 'In Hunza we do not need weapons,
no swords, no guns, no violence. We have one and

only weapon – which each child proudly carries, a pen and a book!' I salute that thought. If only this thought prevails throughout Pakistan.

I left my water bottle somewhere near the fort, my precious mountain water container!   When we returned from the fort almost 45 minutes later, I asked him if he happened to spot it lying somewhere. He grinned proudly, 'you will never misplace anything in Hunza', as he handed me my black steel flask.

Altit Fort is a must visit. The history, the view, the royal garden with grape vines, the wood workshop run by women and **Café Khabasa**, run by local women. Altit Fort is around 1100 years old, which makes it the oldest monument in the Gilgit–Baltistan, dwelling of the hereditary rulers of the Hunza state who carried the title Mir.

Next stop was to find the best place to have Hunza's traditional food. But before that we had to a debt to pay. So we took a local car cab to locate a functioning ATM. To our surprise the guy refused to take back the money he loaned us. Touched by such generosity we ended up convincing him to take the money so we could be at peace. Just then I spotted dried Juniper needles in a clay bowl. He wanted to gift us some but unfortunately could not find it in his storage area.

Juniper Needles

Juniper is an evergreen shrub found on mountains. The tree grows to a height of 6-25 ft (2-8 m) and has stiff, pointed needles that grow to 0.4 in (1 cm) long. The female bears' cones that produce small round bluish-black berries, which take three years to fully mature. Juniper belongs to the pine family. It has diuretic, antiseptic, stomachic, antimicrobial, anti-inflammatory, and anti-rheumatic properties. The tree's therapeutic properties stem from a volatile oil found in the berries. This oil contains terpenes, flavonoid glycosides, tannins, sugar, tar, and resin. (*Google for more information*)

Starving as we were, the kind gentleman earlier had suggested we eat at **Hidden Paradise** which was the best option for local food, all in one place. The owner and chef here, is well known for being the founder of Hunza traditional healthy food. As you enter the antique door of **Hidden Paradise** you are greeted with a large fruit bearing apricot tree. We tried sitting under its shade but the fruit kept falling on our heads! A chance to have a meal to remember for a life time, I wanted to eat what Hunza is famous for. Looking carefully at the menu and doubting my skills to make the wrong order it was best to ask the people themselves for recommendation. We ended up ordering ***Chapshuro*** – a whole wheat chappati wrapped around meat, vegetables and spices baked in oven, often referred to as Hunza's pizza. We chose chicken. Also we ordered ***Mulida Chhagurum*** – chappatis are crushed together mixed with onion, local yogurt, apricot oil and served cold. Unquestionably I had to order dried apricot juice, which I did – twice! There were two European tourists next to our table looking for recommendations and I cordially suggested to one of them that this is a must-try, must-have beverage. Their acknowledgement made me feel like I belong to Hunza! Just a tad too much...!

Must-try food at Hidden Paradise:
*   **Burus Barikutz** (Local soft goat cheese mixed with onion coriander and mint, sandwiched between chappatis, lightly brushed with apricot oil)
*   **Tzamik Potatoes** (A creamy dish of potatoes cooked with crushed apricot kernels)
*   **Dawdo Soup** (Soup with stripped chappatis)

* **Chamus** (Sun-dried organic apricot juice known as Chamus in Hunza. Dried apricots soaked in water for a few hours and blended well)

* **Tip:** Consume as much fresh fruit as possible.

3 days and 2 nights just did not seem enough in Hunza. Knowing it was the last day in Hunza saddened me but there was still plenty of time to embrace the beauty around.

The plan for the day which we were missing was:
Hike up to Hopper Glacier, enjoy the glacier view & all high mountains around, hike down & drive back to Hunza Karimabad for lunch, drive to Duikar for sunset and better view of all the high mountains & the valley,
Enjoy breathtaking view of Karakoram Mountains on the trek, Rakaposhi-7785m, Diran Peak-7200m, Spantik/Golden Peak-7027m, Ultar Peak-7344m and the hopper glacier.

But getting to know the place, people, their lives and their stories seemed more precious in that moment. The Hussaini suspension bridge, Altit Fort, Hopper glacier, and Eagle's nest were all on my list, which fortunately I managed to cover it all in my next trip a year after.

The plan for the evening was to visit Café de Pamir's CEO, Karim Bhai's home. We strolled around until the time came for us to visit Karim bhai's home. My son had made friends with a French lady Jacqueline Lissogoroff, who was working along Karim bhai in his library tucked away between his home and his home-like guesthouse. This lady spends a couple of months helping Karim bhai and his family and insists 'Hunza is not a part of Pakistan'; which you end up agreeing with for various reasons. We followed the floral path down the guesthouse to a welcoming home and many smiling faces.

Karim bhai's son Kamil was out playing but his other three children Komal, Kiran and the little baby Rajab were home. My son who enjoys making friends more so than me, took little time to interact and made friends with the girls and managed to sneak out. Kiran, the third one was the most spirited child in the household. Karim bhai has an auditorium in her name - **Kiran Auditorium Hunza**. We spent a little more than half an hour chit chatting, devouring fresh black cherries and playing with Karim bhai's two little ones. We bid farewell to the finest and most courteously respectful family after sometime. Karim bhai himself is a simple unpretentious gentleman, and his life is inspirational.

In his own words:

When I was 12, I moved to Karachi. I left home with the intention to work and study simultaneously. I started working in a restaurant in Karachi behind the Agha Khan Hospital. I would serve food in the evening while taking orders from AKU and delivering food to the male and female hostels there. Later I developed an interest in typing. To pursue my passion I joined a famous institute at that time when Noor sahib only had 2 or 3 typewriters. Later it expanded to a very famous institute / college under his name. This got me a very good job in the community as a typist. I completed my graduation in Karachi and left for Lahore. Here I joined a tourism company Karavan Leaders as a tour guide in 1998 to almost 2000. Foreign tourism was better in those days therefore we were encouraged to learn a foreign language as an advantage to what we did.

I had keen interest in learning French so I did a years' diploma in 2000 in the language from NIML institute (National Institute of Modern Languages) now NUML (National University of Modern Languages). We used to take trekking groups for trips up on the mountains and have discussions in the evenings, exchange our life stories. On one of these trips I met

Jacqueline Lissogoroff (the lady my son had made friends with earlier). *She was very touched, very moved by my story and offered me to study in Paris. I was obviously overwhelmed. But this wasn't the first time someone had offered for me to visit the foreign land. However, unlike others she kept her promise only because she saw my enthusiasm and passion to study. It meant a lot to me. She took care of everything, from submitting my documents to my admission to invitation letters, visa etc. I left in 2004 and returned 3 years later in 2007. I worked in a hotel alongside my studies. Even though I had every chance of settling there but I wished to return home and serve my people. Here I bought a land which was accidental. Interestingly, a student was going abroad from Islamabad and his mother wanted to sell the property urgently. The boy who got his visa needed money without further delay. So I ended up buying the land in order to help the mother in need. This place is where I needed to carry out my potentials.*

I planned and decided to do something for girl students as they often come here from Upper Hunza valley (Central Hunza) to study further. So I decided to build a girls hostel in order to give them a comfortable accommodation. For five years since 2009 I ran this place as a hostel, with more than 600 registered students. I had planned an accommodation for 80 – 90 students at a time which included almost around 10 – 12 orphans and underprivileged students too. Their accommodation, food and living expense would not be charged for. Since 2014 the locals started building schools in Upper Hunza valley. And the government and privately run colleges were up to intermediate level therefore flow of studies for students ended.

I then planned to turn this place into a café, guesthouse and training center. I run free programs for the community people here. The community run schools can use my space for free for any workshop, lectures or events. People who wish to conduct workshops, lectures or any sort of instructive program for adults or children with special needs can be organized here free of cost.

Back to my café business, my intention was to provide a home-like place for families with children who wish to stay comfortably when visiting Aliabad Hunza (which he has precisely achieved – as my 5 year old declared and referred to it as home). The décor is simple with things we use on daily basis such as baskets and roti platters – things that exclusively define our culture.

As a student I have done odd jobs at hotels in Karachi and in Paris since cooking was my childhood dream and passion. I enjoy cooking at home as well. Therefore today I planned to give my team a rest and cook, ever since Eid they have not rested at all. My nephews are coming all the way from the village to help me as well. As people here are very respectful and it all starts from home. In my family I have supported many children's education since education means a lot to us.

*In my lifetime I have done something that gives me immense pride. As a tour guide I visited Chitral**. There is a village called Broghil (Broghol) in Chitral an undeveloped village, a valley in the north of Chitral district, which flanks Afghanistan's Wakhan corridor. There are approximately 15 – 20 villages there. Access to Broghil is not an easy feat with an incredibly difficult terrain. There I got to interact with a couple of families. I was saddened and concerned about the poor conditions they lived in. The girls in the village would hardly reach grade 5 and be married off. One family that I would stay often with and had grown close to had become like my own family. I proposed that I wanted his daughter, who was in grade 4 at that time, to study further. I was ready to sponsor her, take her responsibility assuring them that I will not disappoint them. I brought her here (with no resistance from her family) and last year she completed her graduation. She has the honour to be* *the first graduate of Broghil Valley. I sent her back with the promise that she will go back home and serve them, teach them. She is an inspiration for the entire Valley.*

Now to complete her education I sent her to Hazara University. She will complete her Masters from there – InshaAllah. She will be the first of her kind in her village. She is like my own child, I raised her, educated her that way. I support and fund education one–hundred percent, whether it is within my family or outside. People earn to educate their children here. You will not find a beggar or a needy person in Hunza valley. They all help each other; no one in this valley is without support. Every one tends to each other's needs. Our community is very strong. I am from Upper Hunza Valley but living in the Central. Religion is very important to me. I am also a Qari so I am always there at funerals; basically we are like a close knit family. The best thing about our community here is we prepare and teach our children and strengthen Leadership skills, once they turn 3. They control the flow of people at the community center. Girls are guides and boys are scouts or volunteers. They each have different uniforms. They are trained to serve food and water, precede crowd in a proper queue – this discipline helps them when they grow up.

My children are already involved in community work. My daughter Komal is a guide and my son Kamil is a scout. They go to the religious school at the community center daily (separate for children & adults) and every Friday they are given their duties. I just want them to complete their studies InshaAllah. Family is very important; I have been happily married since 2001. Fights, arguments, divorce in this part of Gilgit is not a norm. We have an arbitration board so if there are arguments over land etc. people confer their matters there. None of our cases go to the stations or courts. There is Police Station but no prisons here. Prisons are in Gilgit!

** Chitral which is the largest district in the Khyber-Pakhtunkhwa province of Pakistan covers an area of 14,850 km. It is the northernmost district of Pakistan. It shares a border with Gilgit-Baltistan to the east, with Kunar, Badakshan and Nuristan provinces of Afghanistan to the north and west, and with the Khyber-Pakhtunkhwa districts of Swat and Dir to the south. A narrow strip of Wakhan Corridor separates Chitral from Tajikistan in the north.

You talk to him once and you can feel how grateful he is for everything he has been bestowed with. How modest, humble and thankful he is. He speaks highly of Karachi which is appreciable. Suffice it to say, the mountains are gigantic and treacherous, the people warm and touching.

Main attractions of Hunza:

Duikar is Hunza's highest village at an altitude of 2850 meters is almost 2.5 hours walk from Karimabad. Also known as Eagle's Nest, you can view the charming sunset over Rakaposhi, Golden Peak, Diran, Lady Finger and Ultar Peaks.

Hussaini Suspension Bridge located at 45 kms from Aliabad Hunza, hangs over Hunza River in Gojal, Upper Hunza. Predictably the most dangerous oscillation bridge due to the gaps between the wooden planks and I dared cross it, the following year.

Batura, Passu, Hopper, Hisper Glacier is 35 kms from Karimabad while the Hopper and Hisper glaciers are 25 kms away. The journey takes two hours by jeep and the last two kilometers have to be traveled on foot.

Hooper Glacier is a must visit, the village that leads up to the glacier is a gorgeous sight laced with fruit orchards. You will find semi-precious gem shops at the foot of the way leading up to the glacier.

Altit Fort is situated in the village of Altit about three kilometres from Karimabad. It has been built on a sheer rock cliff that falls 300 meters (1,000 feet) into the Indus River. The fort is a100 years older than the Baltit Fort and was at one time inhabited by the ruling family.

This exotic place has several high peaks rise above 6,000 m in the surroundings of Hunza valley. The valley provides spectacular views of some of the most beautiful and magnificent mountains of the world which include:

Rakaposhi 7,788 m (25,551 ft), Ultar Sar 7,388 m (24,239 ft), Bojahagur Duanasir II 7,329 m (24,045 ft), Ghenta Peak 7,090 m (15,631 ft), Hunza Peak 6,270 m (20,571 ft), Darmyani Peak 6,090 m (19,980 ft), and Bublimating (Ladyfinger Peak) 6,000 m (19,685 ft).

The fairy-tale like castle of Baltit, above Karimabad, is a Hanza landmark built about 600 years ago. Stilted on massive legs, its wooden bay windows look out over the valley. Originally, it was used the resistance of the Mirs (the title of the former rulers) of Hunza.

Hunza Valley is also host to the ancient watch towers in Ganish , Baltit Fort and Altit Fort. Watch towers are located in heart of Ganish Village; Baltit Fort stands on top of Karimabad whereas Altit Fort lies at the bottom of the valley. Dating back to 8th century AD, a huge Buddha figure surrounded by small Bodhisattvas is carved on a rock. Pre-historic men and animal figures are carved on rocks along the valley. **Borith Lake** is located in upper Hunza and **Rush Lake** is located near Nagar. The valley is popularly believed to be the inspiration for the mythical valley of Shangri-la in James Hilton's 1933 novel Lost Horizon. As one travels up on the Karakoram Highway, the beautiful sceneries keep on revealing themselves.

On the way one can witness the 65 km long **Batura glacier**, the second longest in Pakistan, surround by Shishper, Batura and Kumpirdior peaks. On reaching Sost one can continue the journey up to Khunjerab or turn west to witness the mystic beauty of Chipursan valley. Chipursan valley has some of most exotic tourist spots in the area. In Yarzirich you can have a look at the majestic Kundahill peak (6000 m), or trek along the Rishepzhurav to the Kundahill to experience the soothing sceneries. Beyond Yazirich you can travel further to Lupghar, Raminj, Reshit, Yeshkook up to Baba Ghundi, the shrine of Baba Ghund, a saint from Afghanistan near the border between Pakistan and Wakhan region of Afghanistan. *(Taken from various sources over the Internet)*

This was by far the longest day of our trip and the most memorable one too. We decided to do something special – so we offered to help Karim bhai and his team in their kitchen. Their special pizza chef Amin Xon and Karim bhai accepted our candid offer and let us chop, slice, blend and almost cook. It was something I never anticipated I had attempt. So we sliced up the vegetables for the Hunza spiced Chinese dish and *raita* - a South Asian dish consisting of yogurt with very small pieces of raw (uncooked) vegetables mixed in.

<u>Raita Recipe</u> (the Hunza way)
   Yogurt (beat well with the beater)
   Chop vegetables using a chopper (cucumber – onion – carrot)
   Mix all vegetables in yogurt.
   Add water to make the *raita* slightly runny. Season it with salt – black pepper and shaan chaat masala.

In the dimly lit guesthouse I mistakenly put S*haan tikka masala* instead of the *chaat masala*, which the good natured Karim bhai said to be quiet about! Amin prepared this crepe like thing which they serve glazed with apricot oil. Being fond of apricots I appreciate anything made out of apricots – oil – juice – soap, fresh & dried apricots! My son and I savored the very unusually tasting crepe, thinly layered with slightly bitter tasting apricot oil. I treasure anything I am offered in the mountains that I would not find in my city. A valuable lesson I want my son to learn to respect, appreciate and be grateful. A year after these guys opened up an eminent pizza place in Karimabad Hunza – Pizza Pamir, the only place that bakes the finest pizza in Karimabad. Amin Xon with his team prepares delicious tasting pizza with special mountain herbs. He is humble, friendly and very courteous.

We spent our last night in Hunza chit chatting under the apricot tree having coffee – the silence of the night which is hard to find in the city.
2 staple must haves in Hunza are:

Arzooq: Home-made, deep-fried donuts / bread. Choose your flavor, plain, sweet or savory: honey, jam, chocolate, fresh cream, herby yogurt cream cheese, thyme, chocolate, or simply dip them in apricot oil or local butter.

Buckwheat Crepes: Thin buckwheat pancakes made with a French- style crepe machine. Have it plain or choose your filling (chocolate, banana, jam, honey, cream, flaxseed butter, maple syrup and fresh seasonal fruit).

Day 06 – The Last Day 14th July 2016

Plan: Breakfast & drive back to Naran (9hrs), Dinner & overnight stay.

We Left Hunza early morning after breakfast with a sad heart. By 7 a.m. we were on the road en route for Batakundi – our last stop. You see these interesting signs on the roads; "Speed thrill but kills" – "It is hilly, do not be silly!" "Life does not rewind! Say no to drugs!"

By 9:30 we reached the Confluence point where the three Mightiest Monutain Ranges meet. The Karakoram, the Hindukush and the Himalayan mountain ranges meet at the confluence of Indus River and the Gilgit River. East across the Indus is the Himalayas, Karakoram lays in the North and Hindukush rests in the West.

The **Himalayas** are about 2,400 km long and runs through India, China, Nepal and Bhutan. The Western Himalayan Range is situated in Kashmir valley and Northern Pakistan, to the south and east of Indus River, and is dominated by Nanga Parbat – worlds ninth highest and known as the "killer" mountain Nanga Parbat is the western most anchor of the western Himalayas.

The **Karakoram** is about 500 km long, lies mostly in Gilgit Baltistan. The southern boundary of the Karakoram is formed, west to east, by the Gilgit, Indus, and Shyok Rivers, which separates the range from the northwestern end of the Himalaya Range. Karakoram Range has more than 60 peaks which are above 7,000 meters (22,960 ft). This range includes K2, which is the second highest peak of the world standing at 8,611 meters (28,251 ft). The other five peaks are named as K1 (Masherbrum), K3 (Broad

Peak), K4 (Gasherbrum II) and K5 (Gasherbrum I). The Siachen Glacier at 70 km and the Biafo Glacier at 63 km rank as the world's second and third longest glaciers outside the Polar Regions. Due to its scenic beauty this the most popular range amongst foreigners and trekkers.

The **Hindukush** range is 966 km long and straddles between Pakistan and Afghanistan. Most parts of the high Hindukush range (Eastern Hindukush range), are located in northern Pakistan and Afghanistan. This range is also present in Ghizar, Yasin Valley, and Ishkoman in Pakistans Northern Areas. Tirich Mir (25,230 ft) located in Chitral (25,289 ft) is the highest point in the Hindukush range. Noshaq located at Pak Afghan border is second highest peak of Hindukush Range and is considered the highest peak of Afghanistan.

Nevertheless these mountain ranges also boast more than 100 peaks above 7000 meters and around 700 peaks above 6000 meters. It is here where the Indus River meets the Gilgit River. It originates in Tibet.

Indus River – Father of all Rivers!
The great geographical features of the Northern Areas are mountains, valleys, and rivers – and the great river of the region is the Indus, on which Pakistan depends for its very existence, together with the five rivers that feed the Indus after they cross the Punjab which, not surprisingly, means 'land of five rivers'. The rivers, all feeding into the Indus River via the Panjnad River are the Beas, Chenab, Jhelum, Ravi, and Sutlej. With a length of 3180 kilometres, the Indus is the longest river in the sub-continent and the third largest in terms of volume. It provides the key water resources for most of Pakistan, while, together with its tributaries, it waters the Punjab, which is the agricultural heartland of the country.

The Indus begins in Tibet, far to the east of the Northern Areas, and as it flows northwestwards, it forms the dividing line between the two highest mountain ranges in the world, namely the Karakoram range to the north of the river, and the western Himalayas to the south of it. Along this part of its course, other large rivers carry glacial waters into the main river, as do hundreds of smaller streams and rivers. Some of the most spectacular parts of the course of the Indus are in the vicinity of the Nanga Parbat massif, where the river has carved out gigantic gorges that are between 4,500 and 5,200 metres high. These gorges are implacably awe-inspiring, being deep, dark, rugged, and near-vertical, with the Indus River rushing, surging, and tumbling along below. When the Indus has rounded Nanga Parbat, it gradually bends to the south, until, between Peshawar and Rawalpindi; it leaves the mountains and enters the plains. For the rest of its route to the sea, now enormously wide and slow-moving, it crosses the plains of the Punjab and Sindh.

(Taken from the book: Around Rakaposhi – Life among Muslims in Northern Pakistan by Brian H. Jones)

We reached Babusar Top around midday. Unfortunately this place has lost its charm over the years, extremely crowded, incessant spontaneous construction and litter across as far as eye can see. It is unfortunate what people have done to this place. Littered from one corner to another with such a beautiful view....We spent a good 45 minutes here, having tea, photography and generally exploring the place. Since it was extremely cold, cloudy and foggy we decided to trek the mountain a little but had to leave before reaching the top. The mountains and the Karakoram Highway from the top are breathtaking. We witnessed after effects of earlier landslide here due to extreme weather, on the way large chunks of rocks led us to the picturesque Babusar Top.

Babusar Top is at an elevation of 13700 feet (4,170 m). Also known as Babusar Pass is at the North of the long Kaghan Valley connecting it with Chilas on the Karakoram Highway (KKH). It is the highest point in the Kaghan Valley that can easily be accessed by cars. Babusar Pass connects Gilgit Baltistan with Khyber Pakhtunkhwa province of Pakistan. In Kaghan valley the mountain system is the highest of the area including the Babusar top. This range flanks the right bank of the Kunhar River, contains a peak Malika Parbat of over 17,000 feet, the highest in the district. On the mountains the grasslands are also found where Gujars and other nomads migrate during summer for grazing their sheep, goats and other animals, as it gets really cold here. On the northern side there are mountains which are the extension of the same mountain system as that of Kaghan Mountains. This range diverges from the eastern side at Musa-ka-Musalla a peak (13,378 feet). Similarly at Kaghan, thick forests are found especially on the higher slopes.

This mountain pass being the highest in Kaghan Valley, is always covered with snow but in summer, snow melts so routes are cleared and it mostly rains there. On the right side, there are snow covered peaks of Kashmir, while the north east gives an interesting view of Nanga Parbat, if only it is a clear day. Only four wheeled cars can go ahead from Jalkhud, that is why it takes 4 hours from Naran to reach Babusar Pass. Mid of July up to the end of September the road beyond Naran is open right up to Babusar. Nevertheless movement is restricted during the monsoon and winter seasons, which is uncertain. The Kaghan Valley is at its best during summer (from May to September). One must check weather forecast before traveling towards Babusar.

Babusar Pass is at a distance of 80 km from Naran. Battakundi is at a distance of 16 km from Naran and provides access to Lalazar Plateau, Dodiputsar Lake and Lulusar Lake which is the biggest natural lake in Hazara and the source of Kunhar river.

On our way towards Batakundi we stopped at Lulusar Lake. One of the most scenic lakes I had witnessed on that trip. The place was so serene, so peaceful in the midst of high mountains and greenish meadows.

Lulusar is a group of mountains near the Naran Valley. It is famous for the large lake situated there which is a popular tourist attraction. The lake is at 3,410 m height. This lake is the main source of the Kunhar River, which flows through the entire Kaghan Valley through Jalkhand, Naran Valley, Kaghan, Jared, Paras and Balakot until it joins the Jhelum River. The lake is much bigger than other lakes around the valley, and is surrounded by snowcapped hills, making it a natural tourist attraction. It has a baby lake beside it too. The word "sar" means "lake" in Shina language.

We pretended to have a snow fight with the scrapes of glaciers around the area. The 10 minute road-side ice fight was fun. By evening we reached Batakundi. I fell in love with the villages that we passed by on our way from Babusar to Batakundi. We crossed Gittidas, Besal and headed towards Jalkhud. On our way we made a quick stop to the spectacular Pyala Lake which looks like a bowl, is on the top of the mountain in the district of Jalkhad.

Batakundi is a small town 16 kilometers (km) from Naran and an alternate base to explore the Kaghan Valley. From here you get a view of the meandering snake-like Kunhar River along with lush green mountains and wheat fields. Furthermore, the Lalazar meadows are a one-hour trek across the hill.

The place we decided to stay the night in Batakundi was away from the market place. Huge mountains, river flowing on one side, lush green pastures with cattle around, it was peaceful, relaxing and the best place to conclude the trip. It is a town filled with noise and excitement and felt just like Peshawar. The sounds of jeeps, barbers, workshops, fruit and vegetable vendors and others faded as the sun sets down.

Suddenly the weather changed and the sky became cloudy. It started to drizzle and the temperature lowered. We decided to stay here, relax, walk and explore the place. We bought fresh fruits, apples, apricots & grapes from the little shops by the river. We spent time sitting and clicking pictures by the Kunhar River. By now all of us had become good friends Alhamdulillah. By night time half of the group decided to head to the market and devour trout. Some of us stayed back and chose to play cards, charades etc. And I am truly glad we did.

After dinner we all sat together talked until midnight, which was a good last day bonding time. We were to wake up at 6 am and decided to have breakfast on the way – our last breakfast together, in fact our last meal together that day. Usmania Hotel Kaghan served us with our standard breakfast of paratha and omelette with doodhpatti. We set off for our return journey by half past 9. Crossing the main cities from Kaghan to Kawai – Balakot – Manshera – Abbotabad – Havelian – Haripur – Taxila – Islamabad.

Day 07 – Islamabad here We Come 15th July 2016

Plan: Continue drive back to Islamabad (8hrs) – Lahore (13hrs)

A brief stop at the Khanpur Dam was a refreshing break from the non-stop journey towards Islamabad.

By 5 o'clock we reached Islamabad. It was warm, sunny and a bright evening. My life's most independent cherished trip across the Karakoram Highway had ended with countless, everlasting memories and a beginning of new segments, friendships and experiences in my life.

Islamabad was not the same, life was not the same or so it felt. There seemed to be another purpose in life, something to look forward to every year. And that is where it all began... more places to explore, more people to meet, share stories, discover cultures, lifestyles, norms, civilizations and cuisines.

Dazed, tired and exhausted after our trip that we chose to head to Safa Gold Mall located within Jinnah Super Market Islamabad to freshen up and fill our lunch-deprived bellies.

Day 07 – Back Home 15th July 2016

Karachi – Back home – Carrying the mixed bag of emotions, as I walked past security to experience the puff of intense heat, snapping me back to reality. Back to the humdrum of monotonous city life, devoid of colour, had started to irk me already. I had decided to fight the urge to break out of the tedious routine as often as possible. The peaks, glaciers, rivers, valleys, villages and hospitality of the people of the Karakoram and the Western Himalayas the nostalgic feeling keeps returning.

Karachi – home, business, employment for many is the financial capital of Pakistan and the capital city of Sindh Province. The city has been much admired and holds importance for its location and economic potential. Today, Karachi is the most populous city in the world and also a major seaport to the otherwise landlocked country of Pakistan. Karachi is also well known for its archaeological sites at Thatta, Mohenjo-Daro and Kot Diji.

Epilogue

Over the course of years I have found solace in the mountains – indeed Gilgit being my favourite destination of all, so I decided to write about it first. I can safely say this was one of my top experiences ever.

I have to return. I have to explore. Why can't I become a traveler for life? I ask that question almost every day since my teenage years. Why can't I have an endless supply of wealth to fund my travel expenses? Or shall I try a career in travel? I want to be a global traveler! From this trip onwards I was adamant to make Rayyan's and my remaining life happy and beautiful. Most certainly I will travel and I did more so then I ever have, to the most beautiful parts of Khyber Pakhtun Khuwa, Gilgit Baltistan, Punjab and Sindh.

The general sense I am left with is one of overwhelming generosity and happiness. Overall, Gilgit was a very rewarding travel destination.

Gilgit-Baltistan - The region is home to some of the world's highest mountain ranges. The main ranges are the Karakoram and the western Himalayas. The Pamir Mountains are to the north, and the Hindu Kush lies to the west. Amongst the highest mountains are K2 (Mount Godwin-Austen) and Nanga Parbat, the latter being one of the most feared mountains in the world. Three of the world's longest glaciers outside the Polar Regions are found in G.B.: the Biafo Glacier, the Baltoro Glacier, and the Batura Glacier. In addition to this, several high-altitude lakes are found here as well.

The hub for mountaineering expeditions in the Karakoram Range, deep rooted history, distinctive cuisine, and welcoming charm of the region has made this one of the most unexpectedly fascinating travel experiences I have had.

I will end by saying that documenting this trip has been a great privilege, in large part because of the wonderful people I met along the way – the reason why my son and I keep returning to the mountains every year.